DREAMWORKS
DRAGONS
DEFENDERS OF BERK
COLOURING FUN

BARF AND BELCH

Barf and Belch are in the Mystery Class of dragons because of their unique attack. One head releases a flammable gas and the other releases a spark to ignite it.

HOW TO USE THIS BOOK

Before you begin colouring the scenes, find the hidden icon in each of the pictures. When you spot it, find the matching sticker on your sticker sheets and attach it to page 16.

igloobooks

MIGHTY DRAGONS

Each dragon is unique and has its own method of attack.
Once trained by a rider, a dragon will be a friend for life.

TOOTHLESS

Toothless is a Night Fury dragon and is quite possibly the last of his kind.
He has many special abilities and is one of the fastest-flying dragons on Berk.

STORMFLY

Stormfly is a loyal dragon and is very protective over her rider, Astrid. Stormfly and Astrid love to soar through the skies together.

BARF AND BELCH

Barf and Belch are in the Mystery Class of dragons because of their unique attack. One head releases a flammable gas and the other releases a spark to ignite it.

DRAGON RIDERS

The Dragon Riders love hanging out together swapping
stories about adventures with their dragons.

HOOKFANG

Hookfang is one of Berk's largest dragons with a hidden ability.
If he is cornered, he can coat himself completely in fire for protection.

MEATLUG

Meatlug is a Gronckle, who loves to eat rocks and boulders.
These rocks allow Gronckles to breathe fire in the form of molten lava balls.

RIDER REWARDS

Special symbols have been hidden on each page of this colouring book. Look through the pages to find them. When you have found the symbols, find the stickers on your sticker sheet and place them on the shield below to complete your own dragon-colouring champion shield!